Xà Bông Tắm Chó

Stacey Tran

GRAMMA POETRY

Soap for the Dogs

Soap for the Dogs
by Stacey Tran

Printed in USA
ISBN 978-0-9987362-5-9
First printing
Published by
Gramma Poetry
gramma.press
Distributed by
Small Press Distribution
spdbooks.org

Cover image (film still):
Icing © 1996
Jeanne Dunning

for my parents

Experience has taught us that action in the now is also always necessary. Our children cannot dream unless they live, they cannot live unless they are nourished & who else will feed them the real food without which their dreams will be no different from ours?

—Audre Lorde

Catching Fish With Two Hands

(Banana leaf blower)

Quail egg white
eyes unraveled

Yellow heart
pile of gravel

The body
washes
the body

Chest open
barrel full
of arrows

To walk away
unplagued

Adult man
pours milk
into beer mug

Satisfaction

When you look
to smell fresh

Kneel beside
a glass case
filled with wet grass

Sit with how
it is heavy
to come

Beside the lake

Incense burning

A clean call
from a country
where death is
a wedding gift

Drag the knife
along a dotted line

Time yourself
clapping
underwater

(Waterbed flirtation session)

Heart skips
into rose
colored camo

Extension cord
rests in a pile

An onion asleep
is a congregation

Going home to feed
unanswerable
reservoirs

My father sharpens
his knives
to cut oranges

The mind dips
a white swan
swimming in a green latte

What came first:
a second or its hand?

I is anchored
by its little head

Jaw a compass

A number
that rhymes
with two

Hold my head
beneath the strainer

My hair will catch
laws of warmth
laws of loss

Epitome of impatience
drying on the roof

Jasmine green blossoms
quite good for a luck charm

A bear cry is the sound a bear makes

while feeding baby birds

to comfort them

Half eaten seeds

blow off into the sea

My watch tilts

toward public crying

Question marks

are the wettest

part of my body

A practice space

for mother's basement

overflowing pickle juice

The mind hides

in a gravity

bin half full

with apricot pits

Tongues make the most

effective sporks

Sweet centerfold
I love your
chocolate bunnies

Babylike vowels
munch through plastic

Deep divers
in two
seven layer hearts

(Instances we touch)

Liquids have it easy
inside a shape

Someone is calm

Loss is no disaster

Wet butterfly in eye

Could I drown in that?

A hue so slight

Only caterpillars
desire my kind
of bilingual

I know people
who are good
at looking the
other way

So the other ear
can hear

That soft
color slang

Come over

Touch my things

I am the only
one of us
with salt

Unphased by heat
or by light
made clean

This is how

Dandelions could swallow
a strong swimmer

My water is sometimes thin

My mother refuses to breathe

Sick during the
sunrise

Fireworks unworked

Open to the public

Yes
he's a flower
she's a flower

Watching the river
melt

Big as a hairpin
I pick it up
with two fingers

I wanted to
know I could
navigate
the world

Looking slant
without aid
licking paper

Pushing sticky stuff closer

New sticky stuff

When a rainbow arrives
I am always surprised

Fake Haiku

Intimacy fails

At the absence of my body

You touch your own body & become butter

Do not trust dictionaries or the weather report

Do not think about your banking account while having sex

Let's begin by cutting potatoes

I want us to have something to look forward to

Ghosts take us from cities to angels

From one lonely city to an angel

My lover is putting me through a silent retreat

Designed for compliment recipients

Unable to accept gifts

Forehead canvas for graffitied manifestos

Earnest & earned like lovers' initials in transit

Denoted by pink bus lights & introductions

My pronouns are shipyard, jellyfish & ten

I sorely miss the city

The angels miss me more

I text C—— a poem about a bird with one wing

She replies by mailing me a piece of cloth

Cut from the pillow she sits on to meditate

I recognize myself in the oncoming season

A clipped cattail at dawn

Nonspecific melon cubes

Beside the window

Spring is blossoming

Blossoming: the first act of rot

Do not clasp the stem while the flowers are still yellow

A new double high found between cracks in pavement

A harvest nested in each bite

A retail heart with ribbon

In case, in glass, forgiven

At the tender table yes is an unclassifiable pleasure

Age isn't a thing, it's a balcony

Overlooking the water

Once in awhile, the trees are just green

Soap for the Dogs

This inert stone is nearly as hard to hold as a fish.

—*Francis Ponge*

Flower District

In Los Angeles, J—— took me to the women's spa where we soaked all day in a mugwort bath & napped in a salt sauna. We walked past colorful fruit stands, fabric stores, nail salons, where I imagined becoming an aesthetician, designing underwear, living in a tiny studio apartment without furniture. But how would I come out to my parents as an aesthetician? That I cut my teeth on some sheer fabric? Is there an instrument you've always wanted to play?

How Gold Floats on Water

Tug on my strings. I can't reach past the circuitry of subway systems & homeland security etched into our thumbs. We gain access to rice smell fogging up shower tiles. We pick apart fruit. It's our favorite sport. Spring appears, bouncy on my mother's rings, sparkling as she manipulates sweet flecks of citrus. Float into my mouth. If I hang a piece of lemon above your bed, would you thirst for it or let it dry?

Tiniest Flight of Speech

Cough the sun out of its sky. Letters of the alphabet hurt toward the end. Can we go on without pronouns? There are at least five ways to say "aunt" which depend on age. I tear a page out of the phonebook & place it on my chest. Wind moves through a place other than trees. When we want to learn a language, what we want to say first indicates where our urgencies lie. There is a difference between how lovers speak & how I would tell my mother I love her. You get the accent right because you sing.

Mimus Polyglottos

To Kill a Mockingbird was published in 1960, the year my mother was born. The 1960s—a time of heartbreak & optimism. As a child, I would fall asleep staring into the open bedroom closet where my mother kept her books for ESL classes at the community college. I can still smell the brown leather backpack that held her books.

In eighth grade we were assigned to read *To Kill A Mockingbird* & I went back to my mother's closet to borrow her copy. I wrote my name in permanent marker in a corner of the book cover, so as to claim it was mine, to protect the fact that I am my mother's—her only child—that I am the sole custodian of her narrative & any threads that touch it.

Responsible for carrying my mother's story in my body with a pair of binoculars in the backseat just in case. I fold a map of my first languages for my mother & my future daughter. Last night I stumbled upon a website with photos of confluences around the world, understanding where two bodies of water meet & that eventually they do mix.

The Cook, the Priest,
the Eye Doctor & Her Lover

Women in Vietnam were permitted to own land 500 years before women in America could.

My mother weighed 98 lbs. when she arrived at the refugee camp. There's a black & white photo of her with foam curlers in her hair. In a time & place without money, where'd she get those? Who took that photo of her? It was about a decade after Tippi Hedren brought her aesthetician to Hope Village to teach women the trade of nail art.

My mother has always been practical, scraping the dirt to uncover a single red envelope. She is the moon on a future harvest where trees once appear to bear no fruit. She keeps going to the garden & tending to it, pruning & watering.

I wonder about the secrets she keeps & if they are burdens for her, if her soul is as pure as she claims it is.

How the Garden Will be Used

As she drove, my mother told her grocery list to me so I could write it down:

- nước mắm,

- thịt heo,

- rau muống,

- tương ớt gà

This was her way of teaching me the difference between xương (bone), sườn (pork ribs) & xuân (springtime).

My uncle asked which language my thoughts form in first, one or the other.

What does it mean to have a way to say one thing in a language but not another? How do I convey exactly how red?

The word for "garden" is the same as "to rise" but it is a different song.

My Father is a Machinist

I woke up this morning, understanding what it means to watch you grating
ginger in my parents' kitchen.

Spit All Over Someone With a Mouthful of Milk if You Want to Find Out Something About Their Personality Fast*

We couldn't come up with another name for what this day is.

Let's fold the letters back & forth to spell: They Continue Killing Us.

Someone at the governor's hotel presses up against a marble

bathroom counter while thinking about erasing us tomorrow.

I'm conflicted by the sight of my friend who is wearing a safety pin.

I want to reach across the room. How are you?

My brain, a mashed-up runway of links shared on social media

while I sit in a room filled with books & friends & their dogs

& my head is empty except that I'm Not the Only One Who
    Feels This Way.

On the bus I eavesdrop the way people use their phones.

No one clicks.

We scroll past picture after headline. It's Enough. It's Too Much.

A wire hanger between my shoulders barely holds together a small pain,

reminding me I've been complacent & complicit.

A bell stretches out inside me, tolling my own deafness.

To cross an ocean, my mother & 135 people hid in a fishing boat without

water for days.

When was the last time you thought about your own mother crawling?

The only prayer you say is for rain.

My father hid in his sister's basement for years because he didn't want

to fight.

He didn't believe the jungle was for killing

& became an undocumented citizen in the country he was born.

*Jenny Holzer

In Law

I sit on the couch until my period bleeds through my pants to the cushion. A block of rose petals we wash our bodies with is becoming smaller.

A sliver, our country. Our mouths gather in the crowd like fish bobbing for air.

We, too, need to breathe & build an index of keys to survive by.

Define *survive*.

Boys decide if they are boys before they want to carry a knife & are told to build a fort of snow to sleep in.

I was in the other room when my father told you his father is going blind. You tell me this at the restaurant. The hamhock we are sharing is getting cold.

He never had another man to trust until we found you.

Soap for the Dogs

My father made monthly visits to the Saigon Central Post Office where dozens of wiry young men like him stood around billowing in their idle smoke clouds & oversized white dress shirts, waiting in line for packages. It was his turn to go up to the counter, already aware of what the box contained: a white envelope tucked in between cartons of cigarettes, a box of laundry drying sheets & a few bars of Camay soap, a brand which is now discontinued.

I count on one hand stories like these. I prod for more, not understanding the pain he must feel in recalling these memories. Bars of soap were his idea of how America smelled.

My version of the American smell is not too far off. Cheap hotels with ashtrays on the nightstand, white towels under the white light of the bathroom where I accidentally dropped my mother's ring down the drain. My father would save the little complimentary bars of soap & take them home. He called them soap for the dogs even though we never had dogs & he himself bathed with the soap.

Stock Photo

In my dream last night my father & I were together, walking along a vast winding public garden made of concrete, the walls endlessly lined with lush red bougainvillea. He was smoking cigarettes, which he quit cold turkey as soon as my mother became pregnant with me. He was young & old at the same time. He laughed out loud. He told me I could do whatever I wanted to do in love as long as there is love. We drove in a car like we did when I was young, my feet up on the dashboard & the sun hitting my knees. The shadow of trees moved fast as we passed them on the highway. He was smiling the whole time he drove, looking out into the distance ahead of him. I wonder if this was a vision of my father without trauma. I wonder if this was a version of him that is possible for me to experience.

Fake Haiku

My worst fear is a knife

Falling on an animal

I unfold the dirt from my hand

I wanted to begin again, a common blur of myself

There is something more pink

Growing outside my window

As long as there's a TV I'm happy

There's a slight chance

Someone called for a reference

Is this bibliography full of white people?

I keep refreshing my online banking summary

Nothing changes

I took notes on sleep talking, silence, stupidity

I kept an armpit journal

I promise to send clippings

Age is nothing but a number for pretzels

Age is nothing but a module for oppression

Flowers that weren't blue are blue

What can I do with a $20 bill

Dragging an elevator outside

It won't be photogenic

Are you really window shopping?

Do you need mostly me?

Or just looking through my inbox for constraints?

I paid $7.50 to sleep in a movie theater

Can I come in while you brush your teeth

Pink flower stained

Locked in a bevy of worrisome corners

I turn the river over to rub its belly

Uncertain how long it will take

I learned to walk backwards

Looking for blossoms that blew away

The tongue you flap towards heaven

A lyrical landing pad

Tent poles, gauze, a trampoline

I prop you up

Together in silence

Crickets tick like the heart

Beating too fast through off hours

In between coffee stained tits

We agree to keep going

Toward the tongue you hold closed & cemented

Everywhere gardens & it's me feeling plenty

When you get out of the shower

You are a bowl of water I tip over slightly

Survival#

Over breakfast I describe it to her as green glass hair

Which we braid at the bottom of the sea

In order to go there, first we gather tiny green apples

A necklace of dried lotus seeds around a new bride's neck

Eight cartfuls of longan & lychee, unsweetened

An arm's length of pearl barley laid out on a cloth the width of
    this door we walked through

Five women carrying mung beans in their mouths

Crossing a sea of milk they fed to their children

Each bean softens with her migration through trauma

A handful of dried dates that have fallen from your eyelids

A swimming pool of snow fungus knotted up like a net

A hundred haircuts worth of kelp

My grandfather in his wheelchair eclipsed by a mountain of ginseng

Rock sugar melting gold across the grainy field

We went into the garden to pick out a poison blocker

We saw fish mint

A lizard's tail

A chameleon plant

Your heartleaf

My fishwort

Our bishop's weed

We are tender stalks

A fuzzy palindrome

I'm your upside-down egg

You're my bird's nest soup

She made a promise to keep the stone wet

Silence, a doorway sewn shut

The morning has no eyes, no mouth, no nose

No ears, either, all my pills are the train we missed

Blame no one

Wake up & eat toast like you would

Read a few pages

Ask each other how to become more wet

A visible thread

A mouth open

We have a long way to go

Learning to peel mangoes without fear

Học ăn, học nói

Học gói, học mở

How to eat, how to speak

How to close, how to open

Everything must be learned

I was scolded for incorrectly cutting a mooncake

Here are stems from which multiple leaves may flourish

Obtain seeds through normal channels

Pinch back the growing center

With regular care, it will grow

Thorns edging the leaves won't hurt you

Waking up

Unlocking a page

Stuck to the floor

I could not pick it up with my fingers

Only by the weight of my mind

Would it budge

& become a little more free

I want to be soft when gently pressed between your thumb &
    index finger

A generation eats salt

The future thirsts for water

A father feeds his daughter Costco meatballs in a paper bowl

Her mother splits open a rambutan with her teeth

We made rings out of longan seeds for our tiny fingers

With a shoestring we pulled a piece of bark, an immortal pet

We grow up being taught to eat outside of the box

On summer Zatarains was the only option for rice in California
    grocery stores

A trumpet for a sun

Certainty reincarnated as chicken hearts cooked in bitter greens

Supertop dining room

A man walks down the street at night pulling a cart of steamed peanuts

Drumming a chopstick on a metal lid of the pot

Striking midnight

A List of Herbs I Want You to Taste in My Mind in Another Language

You open the door

We finally leave town

Oranges roll around in the backseat

Oranges roll onto the linoleum

This wasn't meant to be an homage to the person I lost at the mall

& maybe it still isn't

I'm the kid who sat too long in the massage chair at Brookstone

There is only one man who showed me how to fall in love with hardware stores

A place where you texted me a selfie & I replied with a picture of a fire extinguisher

I'm underdressed when I visit you at work

I want to surround you with the smell of a lumber yard & car grease

Kiss you like someone fixing a truck while the grass gets cut

Obviously it is summer

I spin around so fast in the electronics department I accidentally hug a man who isn't my father

How could I mistake a stranger for the person who taught me to use a computer?

In dreams, a pixelated avatar of Vanna White walks across the stage revealing letters one by one

Vanna White's birthday is a day before my mother's birthday in the year my father was born

At a young age I discovered a soft spot for unicode font

Longing for the idea that a single typeface would satisfy the needs of all semantic ambiguity

I owe processing & using & misusing language to the man who met my mother at a refugee

　camp in Malaysia

Where he taught basic English to Vietnamese refugees like himself

Where he'd climb a mountain to pick orchid bulbs for her

Where she made money securing the buttons on other men's shirts

There's a photo of her smiling

She's cutting the head off a catfish to make soup for everyone

She was surviving

Lighting a candle

A stick of incense burning

Held up in the dark in a bowl of rice

I guess that's one way

We all disintegrate in this physical situation

I left home

74

Then blindness

There is nothing in the beautiful room

I let the field next door fall in front of me

My uncle asked me to kiss the island shaped birthmark on his cheek

Birds leave their nests on top of parked cargo trains on the waterfront

I know where I've come from

I've made a list of herbs I want you to taste

I refer to them in my mind in another language

There are ways to describe depth of color also in that language

It would take fewer words

It would last longer

The word for green & blue are the same

It is the same word meaning giving birth or not quite ripe

I think of the ocean

Vivid with you in it

The future is a piece of cloth I lay down on & cut up & sew together

In there sometimes somewhere

Somehow my soul inserts a pale gray

A raw throw of certain color combinations

That could make me come

You too?

Is this what we look for when we go to the Rothko chapel

Or the Turrell Skyspace?

Or outer space?

Or just plain space?

I said I think it is a landscape, too

I go to the pink salt sauna & hope you have found your equivalent rest

I think you are blue

I think you are crying

I think you are a woven basket

I read you the poem about swimming & god

My insides vibrate so big the waves crash out onto the ground

Before language was a violin hanging on the wall

A metronome on the dresser

Moving images from one shelf in the fridge to another shelf in the fridge

A cold metal slide

A LIST OF HERBS I WANT YOU TO TASTE IN MY MIND IN ANOTHER LANGUAGE

Soup that was too hot to eat

Steamed peanuts on New Year's Eve

Someone knocks

The risk of injury

I run & fall into a vent blowing hot air

Clinging on to the idea of adults as safety

Clinging on to a backyard pond with koi fish as a marker of success

The kiddie pool in M——'s front yard where I first saw another girl take her top off

We played Olly Olly Oxen Free until the stars froze in the heat

While we waited for the pound cake to rise we sucked on ice cubes

Hunger was always a theme at the dinner table

We were given fruit names as nicknames

We watched women roll hot coconut candy on their legs

At my grandmother's funeral

I was too young to mourn

I played with candle wax on the tablecloth of her altar

I am here now

I make eggs & think about unemployment & how saying goodbye to a lover is a labor of

removing the papery skin of a garlic clove

I want to protect my friends & the language they make mistakes with

I add salt to the pan of hot oil to quell our fears

So nobody's wife sees the roses in our teeth

I stand in the kitchen crying while sautéing bitter greens which I eat to feel surprised

Even after I betrayed her

My mother gave me watermelon frost to cure my torn lip

When your eyes close up at night

You continue to travel

I can stay in Los Angeles to become an aesthetician

I can speak another language fluently but in that language there is only one way to talk
about gender

I found a place where people talk about TV without shame & put money into jukeboxes

Listening to plants hooked up to cables & wires hooked up to a computer

We are together in a quiet part of a clean street in Chinatown

I think I love wearing t-shirts here

Where the dive bars are just dive bars

In the morning we eat bananas & buckwheat honey

In another language we talk about disease, illness, sex ed, organ failure, music

78

A wish fell down inside my shirt

But I'm not trying to be exact

At the coffee shop I despise people who take the whole jar of honey to their table

Above all this the moon clips its nails

The beauty of poetry is we decide what it means

After the breakup I bought a plant that costs more than a week's worth of groceries

It died

My father would read tabloid headlines out loud to me at the drugstore

He would take me to the barbershop where I read *National Geographic*

Where the barber offered me Nilla wafers & Dum Dum lollipops

My favorite flavor was the mystery flavor with question marks printed on the wrapper

Life's too short to pretend you are too important for pop music

How to use chopsticks was a lesson of how to pick up a marble

I was taking nail clippers to my eyelashes

My aunt clipped her infant's eyelashes while she was asleep

Because they'll grow back even longer, she said

There are types of marbles containing the deep blue sea

The blue moon

A green ghost

A brass bottle

A tinted crystal

Stars in the sky

Domesticated & wild animals

Or even all the colors

In the army they grew their own rice & ate it while looking at a dish of imaginary fish sauce

Have you ever looked at something & imagined what it tastes like as a way to survive?

My aunt cleaned her restaurant with a cheap plastic bottle of holy water

The front door, all the chairs, the parking lot

What was she feeling for?

In the room

In the dark

What do you see inside your eyelids while you are asleep in a dream?

Please do not brush your hair in the restaurant

Please do not wear red to work

Please do not carry a pocket mirror

Do not eat certain things if you want to bear a son

A LIST OF HERBS I WANT YOU TO TASTE IN MY MIND IN ANOTHER LANGUAGE

81

When my mother was pregnant with me she drank tomato juice

She had one vivid hankering for venison, which she'd never eaten before & to this day never has

How do you know you want something you've never tasted?

How the Garden Will Be Used

Swimmer

We push through lies [——] In front of us [——] Tremble [——] Erasure of thirst [——] Salt cures need [——] Tipping the bowl ever so [——] Slightly to see with a tilt [——] When she said soda [——] My teeth hurt [——] So sweet it falls [——] Through fire [——] Alone, tying your shoes [——] This is home [——] This is yours [——] This is where my children will run away [——] Too & ignite [——] An incantation in my name [——] Pushing through [——] Sage in all corners [——] Noodles getting cold in a bowl so big [——] Never overflow only run [——] Dry [——] Here [——] Absorbing [——] Absolving [——] Which bell would be smallest? [——] Most delicate to swallow? [——] Walk away [——] Pedestrian solitude comes with a pairing [——] Long silk pants [——] Worn by girls to school [——] Clean [——] Caught in wheels of bicycles [——] Crossing train tracks [——] Not foreshadowing the flag [——] Wasting [——] Upon a shadow of a wave [——] A held bet [——] A piece of gold string [——] Sewn in the hem of you [——] One way to treat thirst [——] Swim in soil which plants the root [——] Turn away from the part that hurt [——] You nurture [——] Repel [——] The drop of you [——] Rain on a rose

To My Mother /
To My Future Daughter

after Ocean Vuong

The only mockingbird commonly found in North America is the northern

mockingbird (also known as the *Mimus polyglottos*, from the Greek: 'multiple languages').

If you see yourself in a free box on the sidewalk

Pick a flower from the neighbor's wall

If you break a plate by looking at it

Don't walk away until you've cut your finger picking it up

We are all very close to doing this completely right

The store had almost everything we needed to buy

Trust the rumbling of the train in your gut

It is always on time

Unlike my father she was a few minutes late

Draping someone else's blue lace over her eyelids

Cloaking the snow that went up to her knees over her shoulders

The palm trees behind her as a nice idea of America

[Clean streets]

Where you live in an apartment with a stranger

You come home to cook dinner but he ate the fish you saved for yourself

You go to the cemetery to cry because it is quieter than hunger

I, too, found myself there

In a cemetery

Wearing white

The palm trees behind me

Trying to distract the full moon from capturing the perfect version of me

[In love]

I have a hard time catching her myself

      I must confess I've tried writing this poem before

The one where she used a block of cheese as a doorstop

      When she didn't know what else to do with it

I walk to the center of a room

      Where a white piano plays itself

I walk to the center of an attic

      Where she hides out to eat a bundle of silk bananas to herself

I'm learning how to write the beginning of a poem

      Carrying bolts of fabric through a crowded street

[She sets the price]

      She can peel the skin of a mango away from the flesh

& eyeball where the pit rests

[Throw a fire in there]

The day she sat in the passenger seat of a red convertible

Was the night she filled a vase with a single red rose

I stand in the middle of an abandoned street & look up

Recording my youth for you to compare your light against

[That sky]

In the moment of me without you

Before she knew I existed

She learned English by reading *To Kill A Mockingbird*

It was the only book she owned

For many years from my childhood bed

I fell asleep to the sight of its spine on a shelf in the closet

Beside her brown leather backpack

She only had one

    Now we have many

[What's the saying]

    Without a penny to scratch the wind off our backs

Without a word to break in half

    Without a tooth to sharpen her knife on

Which she turns to unlock a light reflecting

    Not on the fork at dinner

[The road]

    Where you go to meet someone after

To kiss them goodnight

    I hope you do not hide

Tặng Mẹ /
Tặng Con Gái Tương Lai

sau Ocean Vuong

Chim nhại chỉ thường thấy ở Bắc Mỹ là chim nhại bắc
(gọi là *polyglottos Mimus*, từ tiếng Hy Lạp: 'nhiều ngôn ngữ').

Nếu nhìn thấy mình trong một hộp miễn phí trên vỉa hè

chọn một bông hoa từ tường nhà hàng xóm

nếu đập vỡ đĩa bằng cách nhìn vào nó

đừng bỏ đi cho đến khi đã cắt ngón tay

mình làm điều này đã rất gần tới chỗ hoàn toàn đúng

cửa hàng đã gần như có mọi thứ cần mua

tin cậy tiếng xe lửa cào trong ruột

luôn luôn đến đúng giờ

không giống cha, mẹ trễ một vài phút

xếp nếp ren màu xanh trên mí mắt

mặc áo choàng tuyết đã ngập tới gối qua vai

những cây cọ phía sau là một ý tưởng đẹp của Mỹ

[đường phố sạch]

mình sống ngày qua ngày ở thành phố lạ với người lạ

về nhà nấu bữa tối nhưng anh ấy đã ăn phần cá của mình dành dụm

mình đến nghĩa trang khóc vì nơi đây yên lặng hơn cồn cào
bụng đói

mình, thấy mình, ở đó

trong một nghĩa trang

mặc trắng

những cây cọ đằng sau

gắng rút khỏi vầng trăng tròn đang chụp bắt phiên bản hoàn hảo của
mình

[đang yêu]

mình trải qua những thời khắc khó nhọc đuổi bắt nàng một mình

phải thú nhận tôi đã ráng viết bài thơ này trước đó

bài thơ nơi nàng đã dùng một hộp phô mai làm cái chặn cửa

khi nàng không biết dùng nó làm gì

mình bước tới giữa phòng

nơi chiếc đàn piano trắng tự chơi

bài hát không tên y như ống sáo không môi

đến giữa một gác mái

nơi nàng giấu mình ăn nải chuối một mình

học cách bắt đầu một bài thơ

mang vải băng qua một đường phố đông đúc

[nàng đặt giá]

trong ngày từ chối một chiếc xe hơi màu đỏ

trong đêm tìm thấy một đoá hồng tình yêu

đứng giữa một đường phố yên tĩnh và nhìn lên

nhớ lại tuổi trẻ để sau này con gái sẽ biết lúc này

trước khi có con

mình đã gọc tiếng Anh bằng sách *To Kill A Mockingbird*

trên chiếc giường thời thơ ấu

nơi mình ngủ thiếp đi khi nhìn thấy quyển sách trong tủ quần áo

khi không có một xu nào để gãi cánh gió

khi không có nổi một chữ tiếng Anh bẻ đôi

làm thế nào tìm cách cho một con dao bén

khi con dao biến thành một chiếc chìa khóa, cuốn tự điển, bản tin dự báo thời tiết

khi ánh sáng phản chiếu vào nĩa tại bữa ăn tối

phải thực hiện một lựa chọn

đi gặp một ai đó

hy vọng mình không phải trốn tránh

Manifesto

a bird bathing outside the chapel

                                                caught in an act of self immolation

                    not a gun but a glass

                        a pen so small in the hand of the page

whose knuckles wrap around

          a minute casually — lifting

                        a sprig of thyme

                                  broken between hooves of water

— an hour a sliver

      — in caslon & jasmine tea

              — I'm reading a version of my mother's narrative

predating her own

— told from a younger

first person's point of view

in one world the first number is unlucky

in another part of the world one must marry on an odd numbered day

— who became so obsessed

printing flowers all over our dinner plates?

— who manicured them neatly

on the tips of our 10 lives? — who cropped the

elongated cuff

away from the red sky — the fury

a drawn curtain

— wine cooked down to an island shade of blue

a slight mist of a stick on a string

blowing the well-water its reminder of safety

Fake Haiku

Graviola virtuosos escape

Alive on their own

Riffing off margin notes

Black seeds in teeth

Hollow hums play equally well

The climate is thick

Our dense growth does not overlap

You hand me a custard apple

Engraved, my initials glimmer

You dear wild

Sweet bull's heart

My softest watch

Asleep on a broadleaf

Flowering several eyelashes to catch

A hammock strung between two bridges

Mãng cầu, yêu cầu

Our fruits often share the same desire

Wishy heights of romance

We reached under the shirt of love

We resisted unbuttoning the heartbreak of the future

No record of your office visit

We slip into a daily performance
Discovering micro-utopias
A matter of loving the wind

I swim backwards in milk when broken

I can't swing from a parachute, impossible, to be exact

Taken from the ground & placed in water

My pronouns are free, heard & floral

Belly button as shiny as a dime

Swirling on the linoleum floor

There's no worse sound than a door

That opens immediately

Once it has closed

In love I wake up first

I sweep the floor

Wherever the grass is long

Bite into a sugar rose

What do you feel?

Who will trim the weeping willow?

I'm in the passenger seat

Balancing a head of lettuce

Between my knees

I climb into your eye & kiss all the hairs

That's gross

So is the future, an easy thing to admit

Soap for the Dogs

"(Instances we touch)" is a revised excerpt from a piece created with & performed by Lindsay Allison Ruoff, Rachel Springer, Emily Goble, Amy Bernstein, & Leena Joshi for Poetry Press Week (Spring 2015).

"A List of Herbs I Want You To Taste In My Mind In Another Language" was a chapbook published by Gramma in 2017.

"To My Mother / To My Future Daughter" is a self-translation, originally written in English and re-written slightly differently in Vietnamese, following the floating/the difficulty between two confluences of languages. You/the reader may see where the two bodies of water meet and then diverge into different directions.

The title of this book is credited to the author's father from his phrase "xà bông tắm chó" which literally translates to "soap (used to) bathe dogs".

I would like to thank the editors of publications where earlier versions of some of these poems appeared: *AJAR Press* (Nhã Thuyền & Kaitlin Rees), *Brooklyn Rail* (Anselm Berrigan), *Cold Cube* (Aidan Fitzgerald & Michael Heck), *diaCRITICS* (Dao Strom), *The Fanzine* (Ed Steck), *Gramma* (DSS & Tyler Brewington), *Pinwheel* (Stephen Danos), *Queen Mob's* (Erik Kennedy), *Susan / The Journal* (Nathan Wade Carter), *Tagvverk* (Xatherin Gonzalez), *Wendy's Subway*, *Zócalo Public Square* (Colette LaBouff).

I'm grateful to the community of writers & artists who have collaborated with me & continue to lift me up; event organizers who've invited me to read at their series & perform in their spaces; my poetry teachers: Michelle Peñaloza, Lucas Bernhardt, John Beer; Danielle Ross, Jonathan Raissi, Roland Dahwen Wu, Becky Win, Sara Sutter, Megan Gomez for friendship, creativity, conversations, questions, observations, support, & encouragement; She Who Has No Master(s): Angie Chau, Dao Strom, Isabelle Thuy Pelaud, Julie Thi Underhill for breaking spaghetti in half & other life lessons; Vi Khi Nao, CL Young, John Colasacco, Donald Dunbar for reading earlier drafts of this book with big hearts; Jeanne Dunning & Jen Bervin for *Icing*; DSS, Gramma, & Western Bridge for making this book with me; my parents & all of my family; Jack, for being so kind, patient, & bright in my life — I love you.

Stacey Tran is from Portland, OR. She is the creator of Tender

Table, a storytelling series about food, family & identity.

staceytran.com